"There is a resonance to *Robbing the Pillars* that is as much dynamite as it is water slipping over stones. A resonance that calls us again and again to a river that has led a hard living, but with each new rain becomes cleansed. You cannot enter this collection without learning about devotion and perseverance. You cannot leave this collection without it resonating in your bones."

–Cameron Scott, author of *The Book of Cold Mountain*

"In *Robbing the Pillars*, Garrigan takes us on a pilgrimage across the rugged terrain of the Siskiyou Mountains in California through the forests of northern Pennsylvania to the highest peak of Katahdin in Maine. Part poetry and part guidebook to the wilderness, this collection provides us a rewarding consideration of place. Blending naturalistic observation, acute description, and a poet's lyricism, *Robbing the Pillars* is bountiful and diverse as the habitats on Earth."

–Crystal S. Gibbins, editor of *Split Rock Review*

"Garrigan's poems, whether about clearing a trail or a Bob Dylan song, continually bring us back to the ways in which the moments we experience in this amazing world are the results of seven takes in a studio, of eons that made the 'broad shoulders of schist and saprolite,' and how the shad at the end of the poet's sharply perceptive line ran a thousand miles to arrive there, weighing 'three pounds / heavy with muscle, forked tail rudder, enough to finish out its journey.' These poems, too, are heavy with muscle, and have come a long way to show us where we are."

–Christian Barter, author of *Bye-Bye Land*

"*Robbing the Pillars* offers poems from Pennsylvania coal mines to Maine mountains, from the Hoh Rainforest to Joshua Tree National Park, poems infused with the natural and unnatural world, as if the poems themselves are aspens or the trail tools Garrigan once lugged through the wildernesses of his lives. Garrigan tells us that this world 'was called / many things in the languages of animals and roc' ̱ 'hings' into beautiful poems that ring likε

–Sean ̱ding Abbey

Robbing

the

Pillars

POEMS

Michael Garrigan

Homebound Publications
Ensuring that the mainstream isn't the only stream.

HOMEBOUND PUBLICATIONS

Ensuring the mainstream isn't the only stream

Postal Box 1442, Pawcatuck, Connecticut 06379-1442
www.homeboundpublications.com

© 2020 · Text by Michael Garrigan

Quantity sales and special discounts are available on quantity purchases by corporations, associations, bookstores and others. For details, contact the publisher or visit wholesalers such as Ingram or Baker & Taylor.

ISBN · 9781947003842
First Edition
Front Cover Image © John Towner
Interior and Cover Designed by Leslie M. Browning

10 9 8 7 6 5 4 3 2 1

For Jess

"There's sap in the trees if you tap 'em
There's blood on the seas if you map 'em"
–Bill Callahan

"We use our saws in self defense and claim beauty
is the marriage of form and content"
–Todd Davis

CONTENTS

II. WATER

III. ROCK

I. DIRT

ECDYSIS

The dead ash drops
its bark free from phloem
in a year a pushed finger will reach heartwood
mashed [free of nutrients]
        [full of emerald ash borers]
        a molt by invasion.

        The antler scrape chest high on pine velvet rubs of lust.

A quiet grasshopper sheds in solitude, becomes part of the hive
now a locust stridulating as it grows in sound and swagger.
        Introvert turned Extrovert.

        How long do we stare at the skin we've shed?

I ate a burrito and drank a beer before noon
I whooped as the last valley out of Davis peeled
by and my shoulders ditched miles of driving, a small placard
marked Maryland's highest point but I was going too fast
down the mountain to abandon the road.

        How long do we stare?

Yesterday I roamed forests and listened to the universe
whisper on wavelengths of brooks, licks, runs, and kills.
Some ran dry then sprung up miles downstream.

Big rock beds scorched thin brown, dusty.
      A finished shedding— a discarded refrain
      a new first line a stutter step
      breath, a deep rhododendron bloom, a new koozie.

      How long?

A stream runs over my feet in the afternoon,
a fire dries them as the sun scatters out of this ravine.
      Frogs, throaty with August humidity,
      fill in under the spruce and maple.

CURVE OF THE KLAMATH

A meteor struck through our campfire
up in the Siskiyou in late October the night before a blizzard.
We swore it set the woods below us on fire
and when we hiked out to the saddle
       that low point between Upper and Lower Devil Peaks
       to watch the valley flame
all we saw were the lambent whispers of distant
cabins and blinking headlights winding
downstream on the curves of the Klamath
and we could feel Shasta looming in the distant dark,
blind to us until the morning. A totem. A specter.

       That meteor split me.

There are singular moments in our lives that uproot us
       that pull us by our stalks and shake us
              just enough to let settle new dirt,
            a new mycelium membrane maybe
         that connects us to a new system of knowledge,
    senses, perception
     a new tint to our melanin, a new way
              to end a sentence

FAT ON LOSS POTENTIAL

Browns and grays blanket the morning
       corn drying on its stalk, northern fronts flatness grown deep,
cairns that rock me back to when we hiked Doubletop Mountain
in pouring rain and stiff steel toe boots to a peak socked
in currents of Maine clouds, our Dickies soaked against skin
      we ate lunch hunched behind
            a slab of granite
            sheltered from wind in a soft
            eddy of pine scent and musk.

We were too skinny to hold that adult fear
of mortgages insurance phones bills commutes
all we had, all we needed—
      A box of Cheez-Its, a peanut butter and jelly sandwich.
      A shit in the wet woods.
      A false peak. A cheek full of beef jerky.

We hiked down to a summer of drinking beer after four
ten hour days and blackfly blood streaked down our necks
after laying rock steps up the face of Katahdin and cutting
      cedar strewn across trail, flakes of wood
      caught in scraggly beards
      fires at night to keep us awake.

I'm not sure I'd make that climb, now.
      Too dangerous. Too slick.

Though wet woods I walk in the mornings carry me back.

Too far from cell service.

Though false river peaks hook my eyes and keep me
drifting downstream.

Too fat on loss potential.

START OF SEASON

From valley to alpine
      a path strikes
swaths of emerald pine
and copses of shimmering aspen.
      I hike it with heavy pack
      axe, crosscut saw
cutting winter-downed trees
      to a tarn tacked to timberline.

Snow melt cascades down
water bars, dips, drainages
      syphon the trail
      saving tread.

A clear walk back home.

35

I sit in mint because it grows back every year.
I burn its dead stalks in April to fend off frost.

I stand under catalpa in the humid stream
of July because it leaves tropical shade.

In winter bare branches reach up
curve down—a parabola
on winter white graph paper
crumpled with ice.

To sit and to stand is to breathe the particles of place.

HOW TO READ A LANDSCAPE

Notice.

      and be aware of a few

         simple rules—

      Water is, eventually, at the lowest point

         and land will, eventually, bend to it

         and it'll usually, eventually, reach bigger water

downstream.

      Watch the trees, even if you don't know their names

         look at the bark and where they usually stand

         and what they gather around, look!

      Thickets are thickets

         and a pain in the ass

         but they tend to border something beautiful

            isn't that how it usually is?

               you'll see.

Notice. The land

      makes sense if you pay it attention.

It isn't ours to write, but to read.

TWIN SISTERS TRAIL

The ferns' fire red underbelly yellowed by low water
and late fall greet us stepping out of maple and oak
into swept-old rolling Appalachians.

The green leaves canopy a trail cut bank along the slide.
  Red blazes on pine
dirt roads of Pennsylvania
a good breakfast for a day in the woods
  someday I'll pull off and rest,
watch suns and moons roll into dew and frost.

Cross Forks to Windfall to Red Ridge.
  Your directions.

Up this high, the ground is soft. Not like
most of Pennsylvania. Didn't turn my ankle once.

The trail curves, gaining elevation as it wraps
itself into Hammersley Ravine.
  No deer. No bear. Just chipmunks.

This morning trout were snatching my woolly bugger
as it dipped and streaked through their water.

From here I see no water, only endless wooded crescents
    and ridgelines
        folding into tired
    Paleozoic plate shifts.

Tonight we'll make fajitas over fire, but right now
    it's you, me, our dog
standing in the middle of this old burn—1964—
small birch stained yellow by October, groves of ferns,
teaberry popped between molars,
dark streaks on rock nestled in small thorns
eyes closed, a wind comes from deep
sweeps mouth, chills sweat on hair at the edge
of our ears.
This taste settles in my tonsils.

DIRT ROADS AND RAVINES

What has brought me here?
       The deep curve in the northeast
       corner of the question mark
always a step away ready to take my weight.

Slanted letters shaped
       by dirt roads and ravines.
          Bends mirror roads
long slices of rock carving
          cutting deep into dirt
       hiding dark runs
          still waking from winter.

My eyes catch another undercut
bank down at the bottom
a long stretch of water
another question
a curve to
follow.

NEBRASKA, FOURTH OF JULY

16 hours of driving with Wyoming
30 some miles west
12 dollar donation suggested to camp,
Bluestem grass buttress clusters of maple, cottonwood
      caravans of campers curled along
      jet ski cut lake paths. We circled two, three times
before pulling off into a field
      furthest from the noise
unfurling over train tracks and a horizon
stretched like cracked palms caked
in prairie sandweed and penstemon dusk.

We ate with our feet covered in tall grass,
fireworks shot off water and split
the milky way in twos, threes, splashes
of burst color. Trains every hour.

It was cold that night.
I got up in the middle of it
and pissed out a spiraled river
      of dust and buffalo grass
      I stared at those stars
      and fell asleep standing up
my toes dug into soft sandy dirt
a campfire burning in the periphery,
independence day cooked into the sky

    splattered armpit hair dried
    in early summer breeze, nipples hardened
hirsute covering chest and stomach
felt so clean washed in the ethereal
    July of Nebraska.

AT THE HOH RAINFOREST

Each day I button one less button,
My shirt is wide open,
Each day I slip into flip flops,
My feet are caked in two-thousand-mile dirt.

There's always a blue hue,
in the day it's in the water
at night it's in the sky.

Bearded moss drips from branches
Twelve elk cross the river at dusk.

We sleep on a bank cut steep from the spring deluge.

FROZEN ANTLERS

Snow covers the banks at least three feet deep.
Melted, refroze.
      Sometimes I stand at the middle of trees
sometimes I sink in.

Walking downstream in search of feeding trout
An antler tip sticks through the ice.

I've always wanted to find an antler rack
in the woods. A relic fallen off a beast.
      A wild totem
I could look at while sipping tea
      or hang hats off of.

Reaching down, brushing off the snow.
      I grab and yank
Back and forth. Back and forth.
Breaking crust of early spring melt

      Just today I got a letter
      from an old love.
      She asked me about books,
      bikes, and poetry.
      Memories, long frozen and forgotten, began to thaw.

the antler stuck to the carcass
not fully decomposed, frozen since death.

By spring it will be ridden with maggots.
With no knife to cut the antler off and giving it one last kick,
I turn back downstream.
      There's a deep hole at the bend
That looks to hold trout.

COLLIERY

I am always searching
for those abandoned
factories and collieries
my father played
in as a kid.

Every railroad tie I try to walk on—
        never a perfect cadence—
is a reach back for him.

There are things I'd like
to say to him that only young
boys can say to each other.

Gravel and rusted rail spikes,
the faint Morse code of trains in the distance,
the syllables of our shared love.

PYRISCENCE

Some say we must burn to be born
       in fires that break the casing of our seed.
Others say that it's only a matter of stepping
       in the right footprints, yet neither means anything
without smoke signals of our endonym, ashes of our origin.

Sycamore and ailanthus freckle fields
       of strewn boulders, nubs of burnt matches,
and easily mask the gash marks of extraction,
       roots take hold firmly in tires,
sucking nutrients from cigarette butt soil.

My fingers reach into the old fires,
       grab hold of broken glass dirt
covering a contorted tarp strangled by flood waters.
       A weathered smile. Elderberry shoots
prick the ground. I trace turkey tracks along rail beds.

DYLAN'S SLEEVES

There are three takes of "Tangled Up in Blue"
    where you can hear the buttons of his loose cuffs
tapping against the rosewood guitar
    as he strums
           percussive brush strokes
just a bit behind
              just a bit in front
              of each chord.

Each take is slightly singular
    with a blues riff in one as he works the progression
    and a change in pronoun and inflection,
    a quick cut in another
    and then, finally, a full take of seven verses
the only constant are those buttons against the guitar.

I like to think those buttons tapped on his coffee cup
that morning and began the melody and maybe
he wore that shirt out to dinner that night
and those buttons clinked on a bottle of wine
and maybe he donated it to the Salvation Army
and now that rhythm and those pronouns, a bit of the story,
are wrapped around someone else's wrists tapping out a new
narrative, subconscious bristles at the end
    of sleeves smearing sound
        and color across this fretboard.

INVISIBLE TOPOGRAPHY

A deep wind in my chest
scrapes ribs like trees
across a rusted March sky

subtle rattles, buds breaking currents
warm air expands, rising into breath
cold air sinks heavy, compacting, compressing

      All week long I can't keep my eyes on one thing.

      The geese, working their way back
      read the invisible topography
      riding the uneven heating of surface and air
      stitching the seams of winter and spring.

bringing down dead branches
cleaning ribs of the dead wood
I gather, snapping in two across my knee
splintering bone, breaking my chest open
building a bonfire to bury myself in
a balance of burning currents.

HOW TO SURVIVE A BLIZZARD AT 8,000 FEET

Camp at the saddle between Lower and Upper
Devil Peaks. With first light, walk to the edge
of the lip where the Siskiyou Mountains lay
out like a tattered patchwork quilt, tips of Douglas fir
scratch the arch of your foot, the valley thick with clouds
cover Shasta's legs folded together, sitting straight.

There, off its right shoulder, that's the front that will bring
snow tonight. Last night, a meteor burning the sky in two,
tonight, thick snow laying heavy. Punch the rain
fly so your tent doesn't collapse.

In the morning string up a tarp over the rocks
that will hold the fire and pour your chainsaw
gasoline onto wet manzanita and weeping spruce limbs.

Light the fir pitch that you held between your teeth
and cheek as the meteor streaked, sucking its sweetness.
          Sweetness sometimes turns to fire.

Burn all the downed wood around camp
and drink hot tea—ginger, mint. As the blizzard
tapers and sun splinters clouds,
rub your cheek, notice the stubble of snow
that cracks each time you smile
in the sweet warmth held between
those rocks.

THICKET

a thicket of alder growing in the soft bank
of coniferous loam my leaves map out
and skim the surface of the water after heavy
rain and a chipmunk runs down my spine
       birch keep me awake
on a windy night as my back spoons
the conical spruce my feet gather
around tall grass where crickets crawl
their first and last steps and my heart is in everything
       is in the water
       is in the gravel
       is in the dirt
       is in the thick pattern of lives laid bare
       in the fall covered by my leaves my
       branches cold and naked

PIEDMONT PROVINCE

Lowland.

     Karst valleys
          rock eroded into soil
               limestone and dolomite
     caverns flooded
          into aquifers
low hills tilled bare, corn soy in summer, a white oak, cusps of black
locust breaking field.

Upland.

Broad shoulders of schist and saprolite
         crumbled like dried shit
dissolved gneiss long shelves
stacked onto each other
layered as if the
bottom was
falling
out.

HOME GROUND

Alfisol toes, rock knees strewn
in root, alluvial arm branch, hands silver
maple bowed over elderberry. Crows my eyes,
leaves my hair floating in cold April
swallows, ears water slicing piedmont
valley a chest stretched with furrows
pointed with two cardinals, nipples, buds
of spring. bearded night streaked
with smeared nebula gray.

VIBRATIONS

Seagulls spread like little buoys of fishing net
across a winter field filled with half frozen
      water. A train rides upstream, its rumble
      sends gulls into a synchronized wave of white
tonguing the brown February palette
rolling across short summer corn ghosts
lifting into a swirl its tail folding over its head
      cresting so sharply that the world, all of it,
      crashes down onto the field
      collapsing in on itself settling on broken stalks as the train
      curves through the last stand of maple and walnut.

      We are moved by vibrations
      of what is in the distance
      on rails set down decades ago
      and warmed by motion every few hours.
      We startle at the blast of the horn
      that we know is coming.

DEFROCKED

Seven buttons keep starch shirt closed
stiff cotton collar keeps tie tight
under altar boy robe
heavy linen scratches bare skin.

Buttons by the roadside lost in gravel and purple lovegrass
slinging   across   coffee splattered sky
Pearl inlays, swirls of two coasts—
neon and boardwalk,
rocks and redwoods.

Six buttons clasp cloth to cloth keep
me warm in the mountains, reflect tannic springs
ripples of high desert wind off the back
of fluorescent city lights and dewy golf courses
a wound of green and white striking through brown and red.

Four buttons across the ridge, each fir fastened to each manzanita
stems thread through eyelets
A chest broken free from suburban straps.

Two buttons and the sun reaches down to my belly
a heat that warms its hair
a ginger tea.

No buttons left but loose thread
and a sky dotted with four holes of light
each a fable, a constellation

                        long breath maps short exhale.

Joshua Tree silhouettes of arms outstretched, neck high palms nailed
      to a granite chest, sleeves rolled up past cracked elbows, a flimsy
collar quakes in a breeze that rides on the swell of an ocean yawning
at mountains, of tectonic plates collapsing, spreading legs into coyote
      lynx cholla mule deer, a wind that shreds linen into lichen.

II. WATER

SUHS KWUH HAN UH

Its first spoken name, breath
on tongue, shaped by lips
of Lenape, Siskëwahane.

Long before body and blood, it was called
many things in the languages of animals and rock,
to eels it was Place to Leave to Make More
to shad it was Place to Go Back To
to the spring peepers, even now, it is Wetness that Makes Us Sing
The Allegheny Mountains, they call it Father
The oysters, they named it with their spit.

But with body and blood came
syllables and smelting,
smoke and steel,
bridges and boats.

to raftsmen it was The Murmur and Shimmer
of Water and Moonlight Over Shoulder
to the mills it was Good Flow for Timber
to the furnaces it was Good Route for Canals and Trains
to the canals it was Friend, Mentor
to trains it is Neighbor.

It is This, the water that runs four hundred sixty-four
miles to the Chesapeake, rippled meniscus named
many things, that allows us to breathe sounds into song.

BARREL OF EELS

My grandpa told me back before the dams
he'd take a wooden barrel and carve holes
down the sides curving around nails, sun shone
a kaleidoscope of wooden shadows
and coke oven light on diabase rock,
he'd sink those barrels into the river
small weirs
with bait hung inside, nightcrawlers bloody
chicken livers, eels would squirm their way in
moulded pig iron until the morning,
he'd stand on limestone banks and drag barrels,
thick rope calloused hands shoveled dead skin shad
scales on top of eels oily river snakes
floating then flailing as the water drained
he'd shove his hand down into the jellied
mess and grab one, nail down its head while
he sliced the top seam with a buck knife, skinning
it for the meat smoked over catalpa
and cherry, now it's just flathead catfish
carp mercury those eels tasted so good.

FROZEN RIVER DIALOGUE

For Steve

The river's almost frozen over.
     I saw a couple of kayakers in wetsuits paddle
     out from the Bainbridge boat ramp this morning.
Too cold for that shit.

     A creek ran under this bar and trickled
     into the Susquehanna when raftmen floated
     logs past pig iron furnaces blowing
     ripples of hot smelting smoke.

Before we were 21, with nowhere to go,
     we reached for border water.
Summer nights with the river's teeth
bare from a late season drought, covered in dead whiteflies,
the water still.   The water low.   A carpet of river grass
languidly drooped across a chorus of cicada and cricket.
     Carp in the shallows, catfish in the one deep channel.
     Rods in hand, smokes in pockets, we'd rock jump
          out as far as we could, our feet inevitably slipping
          on the smooth diabase rock
               into water
         Hiding ourselves in the potholes and petroglyphs.
     Chicken livers on hooks,
     coal smoke from Brunner Island,
     a fog welding itself to the ridge

heating up like the embers of a fire blown on by

morning sun.

Now a frozen river creaking and thawing
under our warming pints leaning over the wooden
bar worn with the drunk dialogue of sleeves and people.

Tracks mark the bank between us and the river
trains trample by every hour or so
a soundtrack to our laconic meanderings.

HOW TO RUN THE RAPIDS
AT SHOCKS MILL BRIDGE

In low water paddle river right, count
three trestles from the bank, aim
for the middle, boulders will frame
each pillar. Ride the confluence of Codorus
Creek and the Susquehanna. Follow foam lines.

In high water stay river left,
skirt between Pole Island and the corn
fields cradling purple loosestrife and hibiscus,
count three trestles from the left, the last
one before the rock outcropping that blocks
the fourth and fifth.

Follow foam lines, those mergings of marbled
water, where tributaries meet their end,
where currents collide. Let yourself
ride on the palm of the river.

GLUTEN FREE LAP DANCES

Fog lifts off river banks
        leaving three blinking
yellow lights on a blunted busted arrow
advertising "Gluten Free Lap Dances."
        the "D" barely hangs on.

A confluence of commerce
        blinded by smutty neon gas station lights, water
that floods every spring, a bent knuckle brackish
        floodplain.

River and road split past a peninsula of Fantasy Island,
Athena, and Sheetz where the Juniata backs into the Susquehanna.
        This is the dividing line between lower and upper river.
Upstream gradually narrows and eventually splits
into two branches, the west reaches through Appalachian Mountains
        fingering into the Loyalsock, Lycoming, Pine
        Kettle, the Sinnemahoning.
The main stem mirrors the Delaware before reaching
back into the western edge of the Catskills.

The sex of rivers and concrete
comes from the love making of thick
forests and springs.

NEW TROPICAL PATTERN

I was born on a ridge that now fills with water
a few times each summer. Grass
would turn brown tight with thirst
but now stays lush with drink.   Mushrooms grow.

We gather at bridges to feel the spray
of water crashing into cement
       and to be close to the torrent
       of a new tropical pattern.

Handfuls of good soil
      pushed
          down
               into the Chesapeake
soon farms will be riverbeds, oxbows of grain silos and rotting barns.

It's not that I have to worry about the sump pump
      always running. The hoses leak a bit. I duct tape.
It's that the forests have become muddy. Trees shorter. Water deeper.
      I do not know where to go.

SHAD FLAKES

Sweet bologna and chips, a Straub lager. Sceadd.
Iridescent purple blue shad scales brushed by brackish estuary flicker.

We yearn for the next
       detritus piles, New York, Pennsylvania
       sinking silt behind concrete. It will never reach the bay.
dam.
       a congregation of fish and middle aged men swimming
       and swinging in the Susquehanna
       under bald eagle and cormorant dives.

This river used to run through oyster, to bulge with shad every spring.
       This river is a series of long runs backed up into lakes behind
       walls. This river stutters its way to the Chesapeake,
       ladders and trucks push the spawn upstream
       but that's not how this spread of seed should happen.

Line goes tight as I strip back. A rock.
No. It moves and stays low and rushes upstream
out towards the power lines and my reel spins cutting current
breaking downstream my rod bends bends bends
side pressure and it turns back and inch by inch take in line
tight, flakes of light in the murk
       an American Shad that's run thousands of miles
       through salt water and now is in my hands in fresh

water. a kaleidoscope of sea and river. Three pounds
Heavy with muscle, forked tail rudder,
enough to finish out its journey.

TWO WEEKS OF RAIN

Diluvial days, a dearth of dry sun grass that crumbles
under the weight of a slight breeze and a mantis flicker.

Locusts, frogs, sharp snap of cricket crackles a Mars so close
to the moon they must feel the heat of each other's gravity.

Roots shrug free touching their first breeze
when the waters recede, mud lines mark flood
lines, we marinate in the humid air
waiting for the water table to drop so our toes
stop

                        sinking.

A train lumbers down the track as river rises and laps
at its greased rails. Dead wood and dark blue barrels float their way to
the bay.

We

      spill

            out

                  of ground of river of hammock of porch
                  of garage of brick piles covered in English ivy

                  so our roots don't rot
                  in this saturated soil.

SHARP BOW, BLUNT STERN

Scrapes against tall grass, wooden pilings,
rotted teeth of Appalachian winters.
A foothills pond
frozen Generals fallow
fields of Pickett's Charge
tucked between two cabins, a porch empties into late summer
the bow slices a full moon, leaving a crepuscular wake
the aluminum hull of college kids home for summer
shimmers its way into the darkest corner, deepest spot of water
unable to remember who wore the shirt
draped across its yoke
settling into the sunken July dusk.
The blunt stern of his path
ripples wider, laps the grassy shore.
His sides shake
with the paddle brush
streaking the water
a loon the only answer.

RAIN FLY

We left the rain fly unzipped curled under
itself so we could fall asleep staring
at silhouettes of stars and Joshua Trees.
It was a full moon, remember?
The stars only lasted a few hours
until the desert floor turned on again
this time a pale shade of lead
what was burnt yellow and brown in the day
now a luminal white with the moon carving
out the boulders from a milky way backdrop.
We only had a few hours each week.
Our mouths forceps, our fingers dividers
measuring distance collapsing lines point a
to point b into hourglass torso legs breath
protractors of trails and peaks,
collapsing everything outside of the thin nylon
into a campfire of rubble to lean into
for warmth as we found new finger holds
and reaches. Unzipped rainfly on the edge
of a Grand Canyon snow storm, white
slush on rusty red rock,
in Montana, in Maine, in Japan,
viridian landscapes of endless deserts
crags and alpine lakes and vernal ponds
filled with humid droplets flapped off a nylon tent.

AROUND POLE ISLAND

I saw a big bass jump but you were too far across the riffle
to hear when I yelled Big Bass Just Jumped! so I signed it
BIG, arms moving out around my chest
BASS, crisscross on the narrow purple loosestrife ledge
JUMPED, like I was shooting a basketball even flicked the wrist.

This is how the Susquehannock used to talk at night when the river
ran cool with a full moon and they were hunting deer or catching
eel fires peppering banks lighting up inlets and eddies like lightning
bugs bending the reeds of a harmonica of cicada and this is us
in the hot sun at the end of July scouting water for August.

EAGLE, SALMON

I'm drifting small nymphs through tight seams, he's chucking a six-
inch spoon lure across the *entire-fucking-Penobscot* covering hundreds
of feet *not catching-a-goddamned-thing* he mutters under his breath,
his beanie making for a soft gray knob in afternoon mist. Still raining.
He shakes his head, flicks his rod as I catch another salmon. Mutters.
Grunts. Lights another cigarette. A halt in my line rod bent cork
pressing into palm wrist follows the weight at the end. A glimpse of a
wool hat, the flash of the lure he reels in with a step back to let me play
the fish. A small act of camaraderie. "Hey, watch out for that ..." bald
eagle—talons out, wings spread, she sweeps at the salmon—"...there."
Inches. I swear she could brush her feathers against my fingertips.
Droplets roll off as the salmon shivers in air, line curled on water.
Streaking up into a notch of a pine. The rain stops and clouds dissolve
and Wow, damn, there's the top of Katahdin peaking downstream.
The roar of rapids overtakes him and I and Katahdin and eagle and
salmon. A shove of his wrist into the splash of lure as I step onto the
bank.

DEAD BODIES OF THE SUSQUEHANNA

Early in June little bugs swarm
every light   you breathe
them in as you walk
the banks of the river   they hang
on through morning, die off by lunch
        leaving dead bodies like piles of sugar
at the base of bridge trestles,
remnants to be stirred by the daytime wind.

Too hot for closed windows.
Pulled by televisions and bedside lamps,
they rest in corner cobwebs, flitter across the ceiling
halo to halo huddled on the nightstand by morning.

I wake up and barely remember.
Banks between water hold proof.
Cairns, shades of shucks
hug light poles, linger in window screens,
floating the river.

These walks we take between the tracks
and river filled with dead bodies of the Susquehanna
remind us
of hot oatmeal in a tin cup on a cold morning
of coffee spilled on flip flops
of records played while we heat the tortillas for dinner,

of beer drank around a small fire,
of smoke that keeps gnats away
of barks into the woods at stirrings and rustlings
of her roochiness in the hot air of a summer bedroom
of something lived about to begin its float downstream.

NON-NATIVE INVASIVE SPECIES

She sits in her clothes in the front seat of her '86 forest green Subaru
waiting for cars to take a left past her so she can tell them they can't go
that way—I'm just here to fish, I say through an open window—oh
hun you're welcome to park in front or in back of me.

    A cul-de-sac of stone—a Forest Service kiosk marks its edge.
    "Wilderness"
    "Pack It In, Pack It Out" "DECON AREA Columbia Gas"
    "Backcountry Ethics"

I park in back of her and she tells me to watch out for rattlesnakes, so I
do, and there's rain over in Elkins, she says and I note the dark clouds
coming from the west and she kinda chuckles and waves and wishes
me luck and says that I can walk over the bridge if I want, and I thank
her and walk across the bridge around the red tape then cut down
along a little feeder stream and tie on a Parachute Adams and get it
hooked on a stump and see a thirteen inch wild rainbow trout just
before the thunder then another rumble and I work through another
two riffles or so then walk back downstream.

    A berm of burlap runs across the top of the bank
        to stop gravel from washing into stream, a private company
        boundary on public land laid through a thicket.

It was getting loud, the thunder, which made me think about heading
back—so easy to just start planning—but I see this dry side channel
and walk down the rocks watching for snakes repeating that Smog
song that goes "I am a rock bottom riser thanks to you"—and there's a
nice hemlock log in the stream when I get there so I shove my fly over
toward it and a flash and another cast and the fly dives towards the

bottom and I catch a few more like that coming out of fast runs and darting once the water slows, flattens a bit, and the rain is nice but I mostly stand under a sycamore so as not to get too wet. I don't.

What was here before? Chestnut? Oak? Laurels? Blackberry?
Now—Garlic Mustard. Beech. Tree of Heaven. Red Pine.
Short, thick canopy. A molasses of vines.

I get hungry so I walk back on a trail with shoulder high brambles and I can't see my feet which scares me a bit because of our earlier conversation about rattlesnakes. I make it to the gravel and she's getting a bottled water out of her trunk and she's slouched a bit, those clothes reaching back to sit already, and she mentions she wishes it'd rain a bit longer and I finally notice the yellow vest she's wearing and she must get paid to sit here some six miles back a gravel road by the pipeline construction company to make sure people don't take a left over the bridge because I'm guessing that road is too narrow and the trucks need it all and I wonder if they cut it just to access the ravine further up and I wonder if they suck the water from the headwaters and if that's why I saw so many rocks sticking out and then I notice a sign in front of her car that reads "Non-Native Invasive Species" and wonder what she did before the company came to cut in the pipeline and gave her one of the local jobs—

Three trucks come down across the makeshift bridge
two carrying dirt, one empty of pipes.
Big tires. No birds in the trees.

Did she grow up on a farm that was sold off? Was she a stay at home mom? Maybe she's always been single and this is just another way to be alone another holler to park in along a run so I said Yeah and I have to piss so I stand behind my tailgate and piss and pack up my rod and wave at her as I drive away and she waves back already sitting and drinking her bottled water waiting for the next car and I follow the dust of the trucks out to the main road and take a right back towards Seneca.

RESET

Blown out rivers and frosted windshields.
Ammo box of ashes in frozen ground, rain pelts stained glass
melts primary colors of Catholicism on a canvas of organ ripples
across a sharp steeple. A toast of Black Label in the lobby.

     During trudges through death and muddy malaise
     of the everyday it's best to return to native waters.

Ridge of maple and oak, a cradle of tulip poplar and beech
water runs clear at its lowest point, slowly carving cleaving
sandstone channels into runnels. Brook trout chase black
woolly bugger bends of fiberglass. Shadow casts across silt
stirred with heavy step. I sit where water meets water and sip hot tea.

I lose myself in the hold of a ravine where what is innate
still thrives and finds nooks of nymphs and what is not
is just a cold lash across a beard that warms
enough to remind me that there is.
The sun folds under clouds
of laminar consciousness.

YOUR POEM ABOUT UNICORNS

Here is your poem about unicorns
        I promised you back in March
when the last snowstorm of the year
        socked us in for days.

What did we do with all those hours?
        tried to get pregnant.
        painted the kitchen.

This summer we drove to the Pacific, split
        firewood along the Sol
Duc waves then low tides bleached pebbles dry
small crabs scurried out after broken foam
pieces, driftwood. Streaks across sand.

Back home we took the spare room, filled with bags
of onesies, coloring books, bought a futon to stare at a flat screen.

I return to those eddies of the Sol Duc
on nights I can't sleep.
        Our dog paces back and forth between rooms
        his slight steps across hardwood
slow water circling in a bankside nook.
        This is where we are. Across
            the rapids no way a unicorn
                could cross that current.

PERSIST

The creek skulks
    a sunset of orange
creamsicle rock covered in mine
    spill spit and slobber through
Appalachian Mountains folded into ridges and valleys
    worn thin from erosion,
Creasing a coarse beauty of recovery,
    AMD iron oxide death to a watershed
healed by limestone, brook and brown trout
    build redds in Dunkin Donuts coffee cups
and rock melted from their bellies, along banks of rhododendron
    blooming soggy Long John Silver bags.

HOW TO LISTEN TO A RIVER

The complexity of a riffle
      the puzzle of granite boulders
the downed poplar
      the swallow on the branch overhanging
            the bank.

What you see is a clue as to what you'll hear.
But close your eyes at some point, hopefully
with water running over your ankles
and feel the weight of the downstream pull
and how you sink into the pebbled stream bed.

It is an all-encompassing sound, this river.

WILD BOY RUN

is up to its banks
       larch tangled in huckleberry
morning rain streaks down trailer windows
       a cup of fog pours off
the back of Pine Hill down Graveyard Hollow
       wool yellows lay flat in the valley
stained curtain foliage drapes downstream.

       No locusts or cicadas last night.

DIADROMOUS

Catadromous

A mythical west of riprap peaks
pulls me into an elixir of salt
water trenches, bays of cheap
beer blurry steep stairs relentless
pedals pounding up Pittsburgh
inclines no rock to hide under
no fallen tree to slide along
Hand rolled cigarettes clasped
between chapped lips
currents catch pectoral fins
           under indiscernible storms
                    smoke so deep
           sunlight can't reach
                    eyeshine through thin nylon
           tent walls perched in the San Jacintos
                    the Siskiyou, on granite banks of tarns
           vision blurry in each new water
                    shoulders raw from backpack straps
           heavy with clothes, a book, a journal,
                    a caudal fin relentlessly swaying
           back and forth back and forth
                    I flounder.

Anadromous

A cup of coffee each morning
weekends waxed and waned on water
sometimes a summertime jaunt
to Maine woods. A paycheck every two
weeks, dead batteries, budgets blown
annual floods from hurricanes that clip
us off the coast, from ice jams that thaw
suddenly in fifty degree January afternoons,
from dams that don't release water
quick enough into the bay.
      Deep breaths, dorsal fins
      treading before a final run
      upstream until we hit a dam
            or get pecked by long knife herons,
            clamped by eagle talons
            or we make it to where we started
      and we wait and we are there
      and we leave what there is left of us and water
recedes eelgrass strapped
across rock husks
drying out spent
insides wither
to dirt.

CLEFT LIP

Sometimes I find myself in an enjambment
  of moving water
that's hewed rock in a way that
   reminds me of my father and the cleft lip
he was born with and how   if it hadn't been healed
his life would have been   completely different
and how that would have made my existence dubious let alone
allow me to stand   here in this stream.

And I think about how that cleft lip mirrored the landscape
of his childhood up in the Pennsylvania coal country torn, stripped
of its muscle and scarred, its skin cleaved by machinery digging
into its always open mouth, air and pyrite and water, acid
drainage down the throat of the Susquehanna, into the Chesapeake.

And I think about how he gave me this life and how that scar
is an act of love, in some ways, and a stubbornness is there
in its creases of skin that I don't notice anymore, but still admire.

III. ROCK

ANTHRACITE COUNTRY

Part One: Coney Island Lunch

You wander down the street across the railroad tracks that you gaze
down and see a girl trying to ride her bike across so she doesn't fall
into the sharp side gravel but she ends up just carrying it trying not
to trip and you hold the door for an old gentlemen who doesn't say
a word through his fifth lit cigarette to you and you walk in and see
no menu and the lady behind the counter—she's been working here
longer than you've been alive and now she owns the joint and her
grandson is working the register and getting drinks and he has to work
this Thursday to pay for new tires for his truck—she asks you what
you want and you say "Two Dogs" and she asks "Everything?" and
you say "Yup" and she takes a long thin spatula and smears mustard
and ketchup on the bun and places the hot dog in the cradle of
condiment and smothers chili and onions on top suffocating it in the
Coney Island Special and wraps it in paper that grows translucent with
the silent grease and you thank her and pay and walk back to your
truck and the girl on the bike is gone—she must have escaped that
avalanche of gravel—and you're here trying to retrace your father's
childhood but you can't remember exactly the street he grew up on so
you drive around and you hit a dead end over Shamokin Creek which
you think means "place of eels" in Lenape that still runs burnt orange
with Acid Mine Drainage lifeless everything drowned in chemicals
and your pap told your dad who tells you that back in the day when
they heard a Prohibition Agent was coming F&S Brewery would
open all their valves for all their tanks and there would be a three foot

head of beer on the creek as it ran through town and you turn around and siding is torn down the houses row upon row each street narrow enough just for one car but no One Way signs and some porches have people on them some the banisters are falling and there's a bar on each street but also two churches and the hills are so steep your father must have been so damn strong to ride them to the top to the coal mines where he played with the other kids and almost fell into

Part Two: Culm Piles

Airholes. It is the flood of gravel tumbling into a collapsed mine shaft as he tries to clamber out, surrounded by ridges and valleys of anthracite butchered decades ago left hanging on hooks in a rotted roof colliery covered with ailanthus, sumac, culm piles of rock and shale. Anthracite taken, the rest naked in the air, pyrite meeting oxygen and water—acid mine drainage.

This is what's left of the pillar and breast rooms spread out under Shamokin. My father a little boy scrambling up the cascading collapsing pile of gravel of an abandoned mine. Orange water, streams' headwaters erased, replaced with mine tunnels blasted shut and every time he tries to grab a hold he slips a bit further and waits for the rock to settle until trying again turning grasping, his ankles tiny haulers, his shoes stackers, his chest scraping slowing down. Stop.

My father took me on a tour of the mines when I was a kid and we visited his grandfather, Poppy Augustine. It was dark on the roads and in his room. The linoleum beige, worn dim like those hills, covered in soot. He was dying, laying in a starched hospital bed, skinny with near death and my father asked him to tell us stories. He did. When he was little he was one of the boys that would rob the pillars, setting the explosives since he was small enough to fit those tiny spaces deep in the rock. Their tiny fingers were perfect for the job. They'd run as the fuse crackled and the explosion ruptured the rock. They'd wait for the dust to settle, counting the seconds to see if the mountain was done collapsing or if they'd have to run. Birds, mules, and fires the marks of oxygen. "If they went, you ran," he said. We ate hot dogs. Thank you. This is part of that love. These are our headwaters.

Resource extraction. No one reaches down for him so my father inches up, careful to find his weight on the right rock, dilate, hold still, wait again for the settle. The culm of the company's profit margin. Out of the corner of his eye he sees a copse of trees, hemlocks he thinks, growing tall enough to cover the coal equipment over on Cameron Colliery, once the tallest man made mountain now a blackness spattered by dark green.

And the companies just went bankrupt and left.
But water does not go bankrupt, beech and birch do not go bankrupt Orion does not go bankrupt as he slides his way across the horizon cut with a rusted out Bucyrus Erie dragline still reaching out dangling its bucket over an open pit sore.

My father's hands finally find solid ground. He pulls himself up and stands, his knees, bloodied through torn jeans, burn in thick summer

air like dried leaves languid in diesel smoke. He wipes the dirt from his
cleft lip scar and walks home, down the silent hill to Shamokin Street.

We build small fires, let them smoke out to keep mosquitos
away and in the dark that eventually comes I ask

What was Pap like when he got off work?
How did he tell you he was taking the family
out to Rock Island, Illinois along the Mississippi
so he could become a chiropractor?
Is that river, like these rocks, in my blood?

Part Three: Roaring Creek

I was downstream releasing
a brook trout, holding hundred
years of genes, a survivor of the mining,
when I heard the collar
of a dog walking the trail.

There was nothing for them
to hear of me. No sound
to offer.

NATIVE, WILD, INVASIVE
Marietta, PA

When continents broke and shifted natives
survived spread on wings, safe in eddies and cracks of granite.
Genes stretched over thousands of years, unfathomable generations.

> Brook trout.
> Solomon Seal.
> Oyster, eel, shad.

Wild came after identification and labels,
but now propagate freely.
They have found a niche of coexistence.

> Brown trout.
> Sycamore.
> Carp, bass, jasmine weed.

Invasives have yet to find a balance.
Some will devour until their end.
Some become wild.

> Rainbow trout.
> Japanese knotweed.
> Flatheads, snakeheads, incinerators.

Standing on the cusp of these lines
dictating and determining what survives
and what ends yet we rarely recognize
our own fingertips, their smudges dark
like ash across the horizon.

VESTA FURNACE

Blast furnace born mysticism, molten slag
spread like seed on heels of deer
grazing land tattooed by industry of timber, of rock.
        My prayers subtle twitches of tall grass.
        Crickets scurrying on water.

I kneel at a pig iron altar hugged by sycamore, silver maple,
English ivy wraps my wrists, my waist, brick culm piles
from anthracite fired furnaces a sacristy, a second story canopy.

This water has run across these rocks for more
lifetimes than any conjured deity.
This oyster river is older than the ridges that follow it.
A runnel turned river
when Gondwana slammed into EurAmerica. It has survived
dams, disease, drought, development, and nuclear meltdown.

It will run long after I am gone.
        Its flow a faith in everlasting life.
        Hallowed be thy name. Susquehanna.
A river cleansed with each rain, the shimmer and shake
of little darters through muddy shallows.
Crayfish, minnows. Amen.

LIFE-CAGE

after Robinson Jeffers

I am fine
    with the inevitable

        life and death
            tumble and settle

    with the daily

        to and from
            work and home

    with the faith

        in screens and
            empty gas tanks

    with the scree

        slope of morning
            ravine of nights

    with the quarry

        of the rock
            from the water

    with the capitalization

        of the gods
            and the companies.

It is the after that bothers me, the desire to be remembered.
But that is the wrong word. Not remembered, but useful.
The best things in this life are still useful in this death—
    leaves, roadkill, salmon, antler, orange peels.

Plant me in the moss. Lay me in the sun. Float me in the river.
An afterlife of decomposition into the universal
consciousness of soil and water.
Cleave the grain of each day with the certainty of a useful death.

HOW TO CLIMB KATAHDIN

You have options—
Abol, Katahdin Stream,
Roaring Brook, Chimney Pond —
each leads to the same peak,
each takes its own turns.

It should be dark when you start.
Your pack should have what you need.
Do not get fooled by false peaks.
        That much is obvious.

Here's what's not,
        look for the pink flecks
        mottling the granite
        and the cleave marks
        that break the grain,
        the joining of mineral and color.

The ground holds your balance,
the mountain pushes your heels
into the next step up into scraggly
fir and bilberry, trees turn to tundra,
        the clouds are there, at your lips.

YOU SAID I DIDN'T LIKE RELIGION

Sterling Mountain's bottom lip,
a pond with brook trout frog
croaks and short alpine balsam fir,
blends the southern deciduous
and northern boreal forests.
Deadwood lines the banks,
a notch left over from the collision
of the Canadian Shield with South
America and West Africa once buried
with volcanic ash, scraped clean
by the Laurentide Ice sheet. Dragonflies
hover around my feet on the pebbled shore
3,000 feet high. The water closest
to the sky in the state. My little prayers
of casts out into the dark blue water,
what I imagine my eyes look like
with the first glance of the day,
inhale exhale slow strips of line
will it reach? will it land?
sometimes a halt and a play and a dance
sometimes nothing.

HOLY TRINITY

No more tangled, hung-up mind.
I idly scribble poems on the rock cliff,
Taking whatever comes, like a drifting boat.
                    –Han Shan

Clouds come in over pine,
water spews from dam,
Eagle searches for salmon.

Cedar leans forward
            across eddy. Path turns.
Soft spruce & fir needles silences steps.

            water is water.
            fish is fish.
            rock is rock.

PANTHER HOLLOW

We skipped lectures to sit under Schenley Park
bridges. Stoned, we'd clamber down to Acid
Lake to the edge of iridescent
       colors swirling in late afternoon oily sheen.
       We stared at still water.
       Bass lingered deep at the bottom.

Smoke gathered from rolled cigarettes
piles of rocks, pebbles on concrete
broken from construction
       of Phipps Conservatory
or fallen from the bridge spanning the crevice.
Yellow beams stretched across blue skin.

The largest swath of green we could find.
       Now I look at maps and let my eyes
       land on the green splotches.
There. That's where I want to go.

We skipped rocks through the afternoon
       until dinner and finally, once the sun dipped
          out beyond Panther Hollow,
             we followed the smoky hue of South

Oakland back to our dorms

        those rocks still arcing across water

          the pores of our fingers

            filled with dirt.

I carry it with me.

Smoke still in lungs. Fingers still dirty.

Waiting for that last splash to exhale.

GUARDIAN OF THE MOUNTAINS

Checkpoint #1

We were where desert meets pine to cut
chaparral and clear downed trees.
Santa Ana winds ripped our tents, breathing ice across breakfast
faces blistered by cold sand, buried in a grit cloth.

Checkpoint #2

A borderland desert landscape bounds a quebrada of cottonwoods—
thin grass and a sliver of a stream—in the Hauser Wilderness.
Shirts pants bags baby formula wind
clustered around trees, caught in sage.
Ornaments of Migration.
We drink, Dave's long white hair sticks to his spine.
He nods at the piles, says
I only drink coffee and beer. I carry water for them. I say in Spanish:
Yo soy el guardián de las montañas.
La gente viene aquí para estar más cerca de Dios.
Tengo comida y agua que compartiré contigo.

Checkpoint #3

On day six we stop for lunch along a switchback
after cutting trail all morning and watch
border patrol scurry like recluse spiders
along highways cutting Laguna Mountains.
       Your shoulders covered by a ratty blanket stuck
       with briars, matted with dirt
       you cradle your plastic bottle so the creek water
       won't spill out of the hole.
       Your jeans heavy wet with sweat frozen
       at night thawed each morning.
We give you water and trail mix and beef jerky.
       Did you make it? Or are you bloated gray green?
       Are vultures circling overhead, hide beatles eating
       the hard dried tissue? Did you find your father?
You keep walking north.
We have trail to cut.

TRAIL WORK SUITES

Dry Stone Masonry

I laid rock into patterns up sides of mountains
      for a few years after college.
I learned balance—a rock bar in both hands is easier hiking
      than only one.
I learned weight—one edge can settle onto the thick of another
      to create a strong joint.
I learned depth—a well dug hole shaped in anticipation will hold
      the heft tightly.
I learned erosion—water flowing straight down a mountain
      will carry much sediment.
I learned fill—crushed granite mixes well with small quartz
      and gneiss pebbles create a soft but solid base of support.

I learned this eating beef jerky from my pocket
covered in lint and dust.
I learned this on the cabin porch looking out
over Kidney Pond. Katahdin
sat off to my left and I'd take a glance
after every sip and it was there. Always.
I learned the love for totems, relentlessly present.

Clearing Trail

Chainsaw over shoulder—bar out the back,
chaps tied around engine sitting next to cheek, Kevlar,
bar oil, gasoline in a dry bag, a hand axe, two yellow plastic wedges
just in case, an extra chain and bolt. Ten miles in, ten miles out.

When it's dry the wood chips float across us like duff glitter.

Clearing the sinuses of the woods. Letting ourselves in, just a little.

Wood Bridges

I find two cedar stringers 30 yards off trail.
        Walk backwards, holding the axe until its handle
meets the top of the tree. Mark the fell point
        with a stick, notch them, drop them
with a back cut and two wedges. Skin them, line them out
        with grip hoist and pulleys.
Log carriers get them parallel to trail, cant hooks settle them onto sills.
        Planks pounded in with rebar.
                A dry path to Sandy Stream Pond Trail.

Bog Bridges

Freeze Out Trail off Fish Hawk Road. Last week of September
in Maine. The first hint of winter at night, close to freezing.
Laying 20 sections of bog bridges, clearing pine off trail
      after a summer wind storm.
Short cedar sleepers, six foot planks
      draw knives, bark spuds, thick nails, single jacks.
We work our way through the mud, sinking each step,
we find a cedar root ball to sit on for lunch.

Brushing

Endless ridges of the Siskiyou, Shasta
sitting still just to our south, her head dusted white
in late October snow. Grandma totem.
Hand loppers and saws pruning manzanita
crosscut saws for the errant Douglas
fir. Paths through woods. Those were long days
where I wished for the engine drone to drown
      out the eight-thousand-foot silence.
      We sang Petty songs instead.
A meteor streaked across the sky the night before snow.

GRISTMILL GRAVEYARD

Rock creased with dark shadows of furnace stacks a stream shoved over by concrete trestles. Roots hold thick. Millstones scatter, thrown from the freeway a few broken, some laid up against a stone wall stacked a hundred years ago, some emerge only in July and August drought. A gristmill graveyard. Axes, handle carved, gun-barrels reamed bored moulded. This water turned stone grinding rye and corn to feed the two copper stills on the ridge before they could blast the sides and put in a four-laner 100 feet above the riverbed, striking through the cleave of Appalachian and lowland—sandstone, siltstone, and shale. A narrow hinge rusted shut balanced on plunged folds. Industrial past sliding into a ravine. Scars, sure. No matter. This is our normal. Our baseline ailanthus, thick brambles, macadam. But. There is mountain laurel. There is slack water stacked full of driftwood. There is a trash bag with a bloody deer hoof sticking through. There are wild trout in the water with a road from here to the Juniata to the Susquehanna. Each downstream mile wider, warmer. Hemlocks turn to sycamore. Water runs through gills, grinding run-off soot into breath. Caddis larvae shuck off the streambed.

SEVERANCE TAX

Vultures pick deer carrion in the gravel edge of Route 81
they mean no harm in their clean up but get no love,
their beaks are made for the job they do.

Dragline excavators and drilling rigs fissure the horizon
steel rails and pendulums offer no buds in spring, rust yearlong.
      Anthracite, now Marcellus Shale.

      All—flesh, water, rock, dirt, stem—
      pay a severance tax for existence.

Some of us band together, use language to make lines on paper
to create larger illusory selves that exist yet can't be touched
or handcuffed or kissed or made omelettes on a rainy morning,
becoming an incorporated capital W and E
and fracture geological lines
and shoot water down encased wellbores,
flood the ground, pressure against pressure to rupture gas,
suck it dry, raze whole mountainsides, leaving only
smears of burnt coal and gas
      hazy like an August day even in December. We let
      vultures pick at what's left, and the individual I and lowercase
      we pick up the bill and sweep
      the anthropogenic debris downstream.

GEOLOGICAL THAW

Morning sun breaches trees
lighting a fieldstone hunch
scattered across edges of black locust. Some fall
into Codorus Furnace ravine, some a wall.

Turkey vultures hang on gelid limbs
naked to wind as river moves
spring crawls downstream, fuller,
bloated with turbid snowmelt.

I go into the woods along the river and stare
   silver maples and serviceberry gather
along barked railroad tracks muttering by
webbed geometry of trees in snow
drift me back to when

  I fell asleep on the side of Katahdin
  with a storm blowing
  in thick fog
  mist covered dew all day
  I leaned my head against my Kelty pack.
  hadn't seen my family in months.
  Feldspar curved into my back.
  The closest I've been.

Diurnal falls railroad rubble
riverbank movements water over rock
currents breaking, staving off
the last winter air looking, circling.

34

Dark gravel at five a.m.
covered by a hatch
of sleet and snow.

Empty parking lot.
Rhododendron leans in,
a rainbow trout on a hare's ear nymph.

Working downstream
Bridge to bridge.
Strip, strip, nudge and cast.

Trains lumber through—
freight, oil tankers, passenger cars—
serrated teethy cleaves and glinting sunlight of limestone and shale.

A grove of mid century rust belt ranchers,
white porches splayed with rock salt slush,
ease their end into the valley, the river.

A ferruginous notch slices a path
in the eddies of the Appalachian plateau
like sycamore roots veined in snow.

WHERE IS THIS GOD YOU SPEAK OF?

It was the word "god" that tore me apart
after you said he punishes those that
masturbate. I was 13. I never valued cruelty.

That word packed full of punishment and doubt and trust
but what is there to trust about the injustice of mayflies
caught in a trap of fluorescent flood lights?

That word filled like the low part of a fallow field.
Mud. Moldy stalks. Water spiders flicking across murk.
But I stepped in, I sank and lost my shoe.
     Rubber compost.

And that word. It became
     bike.
     tent.
     ridge.
     cedar.
     coffee.
     herthighs.
     cigarette.
     Siskiyou.
     burrito.
     Nanita.
     Susquehanna.

And I lose language and I follow bats in dusk.

And I crack mint leaves and follow subtle
breezes and the way locust and oak
and sweetgum create a horizon of swaying green.

And god is just another word for now is just another word for
the streak of a dead bug on my windshield and the hawk on that
telephone pole and that cracked skin stretched across the back of my
hand and that thought of Montana that soaks cereal each morning and
that back-up beep of the recycling truck as it gets closer to start its day
at the dead end street outside my bedroom window and I can't hear
it now because the robins cardinals sparrows and bluebirds wake up
earlier and call forth another sun for us mayflies to get caught in.

HOW TO MAKE A MOUNTAIN

Prayer hands push up and break the crust
and dirt and rock tumble across the back
of your hands, but keep the fingers together,
that is your power, that is where you reach
to and once your thumbs are out, flick them
to the side and there, now you have a ravine
and when it rains water will flow and salamanders
will crawl their way around the little pebbles of your knuckles
and there will be a river that rushes by your wrist that cleanses,
that murmurs lines of dialogue and direction. Listen.

DEER MOUNTAIN

Just south of the Canadian border
caddis dimple water lined by thick alder
      last night, a storm
      tonight, the milky way.
Filaments of bearded moss hang still on spruce limbs
      a fire dries my ankles.

What feeds on the sweetness of trees?
      Candy smoke and a sky of sap
pixelated by stars, dries white with streaks
      down bark, a caramel glint scar.

Some see rocks only after trees are cut or bulldozers scrape
or only hear them as thunder strewn on the edge of night.

Some see them by how they move water,
      giving a river and its banks
and its thicket and canopy a rhythm.

There is life under what we cannot see.
Cases of caddis pupa fix to the undersides of rock undulate
off the hard surface into something that floats, then flutters.

ROBBING THE PILLARS

Poppy Augustine crawled into the deepest
part of the Shamokin mines as a kid to rob the pillars,
> drilling holes into the anthracite, placing dynamite
> into walls of stone left to hold up the mountain,
> lighting the fuse and running until he was far enough
> > to sit and wait for the blast
> > > the settle
> > > > the quiet
> > > > > that had to last
at least sixty seconds.   In that silence he made
eye contact with the mule, and if he fell still the oxygen was gone
sucked back to the surface and that meant to chase it. Retreat.
> Once that silence was long enough
> and those breaths taken
he'd grab his short shovel for his short arms and small
hands and start filling the carts with the blasted coal.

> Did he blow out his carbide lamp
> and rest in that dark silence?
> Did he play with dirt between his fingers?
> Did rocks become toy trucks in those
> seconds of possible collapse?

I strand myself in streams and close my eyes
and wait for water crashing collapsing that covers
but does not bury become a silence that settles
onto me the bank the clouds of bugs the breaths of woods
gripping the soil and geology of their seed.

Everything becomes a silence if we give it long enough.

ACKNOWLEDGMENTS

Alternating Current Press, Undeniable: Writers Respond to Climate Change—"New Tropical Pattern"

Barren Magazine—"Where is this god you speak of?"

Deep Wild Journal—"Curve of the Klamath"

Foliate Oak Literary Magazine—"Sharp Bow, Blunt Stern," "Thicket"

Gray's Sporting Journal—"Frozen Antlers"

Hawk and Handsaw Journal—"Barrel of Eels," "Diadromous," "Severance Tax," "Robbing the Pillars"

The Merrimack Review—"Geological Thaw," "Invisible Topography"

Peatsmoke Journal—"You Said I Didn't Like Religion"

Permafrost - "Cleft Lip"

Piedmont Journal of Poetry & Fiction—"34," "Dead Salmon,"

Poets Facing the Wall Anthology, The Raving Press—"Guardian of the Mountains"

Sky Island Journal—"Life-Cage"

Split Rock Review—"Deer Mountain"

Tiny Seed Journal—"Dirt Roads and Ravines"

The Wayfarer—"Dead Bodies of the Susquehanna"

What I Know [How to Do], Finishing Line Press—"How to Climb Katahdin," "How to Listen to a River," "How to Make a Mountain," "How to Read a Landscape," "How to Run the Rapids at Shocks Mill Bridge," "How to Survive a Blizzard at 8,000 Feet"

THANK YOU

My deepest gratitude to my wife, Jessica, for supporting me throughout the writing of these poems. I am incredibly grateful for her critical eye and relentless belief in my work.

To Steve Mohr, always ready to go to the river. Thank you, brother.

To Jeff Debelis, thanks for reminding me what a good poem is and for guiding the revision of many of these poems.

To those who spent time with me on the trail and streamside, thank you for being part of those long songs.

To my family, especially my parents, Nana, and Grandma, thank you for taking me to the roots of our family in the coal regions of Pennsylvania and sharing stories that shaped this collection.

ABOUT THE AUTHOR

Michael Garrigan writes and teaches along the banks of the Susquehanna River in Pennsylvania. He enjoys exploring the river's many tributaries with a fly rod and hiking the riverlands with his wife and dog. His summers are spent in search of wild trout in wild places. He loves watching water move over rocks and feels strongly that every watershed should have a Poet Laureate.

Michael holds a BA in Creative Writing from the University of Pittsburgh and an MA in English & Creative Writing from Southern New Hampshire University. He is the author of the chapbook *What I Know [How to Do]* (Finishing Line Press) and his essays and poetry have appeared in *Gray's Sporting Journal, The Wayfarer, The Drake Magazine, Hawk & Handsaw, Permafrost, Sky Island Journal, Split Rock Review,* and other magazines and anthologies.

You can find more of his writing at www.mgarrigan.com.

HOMEBOUND PUBLICATIONS
POETRY OFFERINGS

———

IF YOU ENJOYED THIS TITLE, PLEASE CONSIDER
THESE COLLECTIONS FROM OUR POETIC LIBRARY:

Joy is the Thinnest Layer by Gunilla Norris

Ruminations at Twilight by L.M. Browning

Having Listened by Gary Whited

Four Blue Eggs by Amy Nawrocki

The Uncallused Hand by Walker Abel

Rolling Up the Sky by Linda Flaherty Haltmaier

Water, Rocks and Trees by James Scott Smith

To Look Out From by Dede Cummings

The School of Soft-Attention by Frank LaRue Owen

After Following by Burt Bradley

A Taste of Water and Stone by Jason Kirkey

Children to the Mountain by Gary Lindorff

Night, Mystery & Light by J.K. McDowell

Rooted & Risen by Timothy P. McLaughlin

Blood Moon by Andrew Jarvis

WWW.HOMEBOUNDPUBLICATIONS.COM
LOOK FOR OUR TITLES WHEREVER BOOKS ARE SOLD

Printed in the USA
CPSIA information can be obtained
at www.ICGtesting.com
JSHW080002150824
68134JS00021B/2235

9 781947 003842